DEDICATION:

To all brides, their mothers, and all necessary planning "others."

Remember your mantra: WHOSE WEDDING IS THIS ANYHOW?
(*NOTES FROM THE M.O.B.*, by Sherri Goodall)

WeddingDetails FAQ's

101 ANSWERS TO YOUR TOP WEDDING PLANNING QUESTIONS

by Sherri Goodall
with experts Edith Gilbert, Lois Pearce, Jeff Allen,
Jack Benoff and Pat Taylor

Published by Pennythought Press
7512 S. Gary Place
Tulsa, Oklahoma 74136

ISBN: 0-9671235-1-8

Cover Photo by Boyd Harris

Printed in the United States of America

Contents

$\mathcal{I}$ntroduction

$\mathcal{I}$t takes an average of 8 days, condensed—without sleep—to plan a wedding. Many of those hours and minutes are spent looking for answers. The "experts" of *weddingdetails.com* have pooled their most frequently asked questions and answers concerning wedding planning into **weddingdetails.com FAQ'S**.

Now you have no further to go than this book, provided you keep it with you!

Sherri, Lois, Edith, Jeff, Pat, and Jack supply the answers to age-old questions that have concerned brides for centuries. In addition, they have the answers to current issues—blended and extended families, alternative lifestyles, and new trends and old traditions.

Six areas of wedding planning are covered in this book:

♥ MOTHER OF THE BRIDE issues by Sherri Goodall...she wrote the book, NOTES FROM THE M.O.B. (Mother of the Bride). Sherri has consulted on hundreds of weddings in her 13 years as a party consultant and has encountered nearly every possible wedding event situation in those years.

♥ ETIQUETTE by Edith Gilbert, one of the wedding industry's most renown wedding consultants; a lecturer and author of several books.

♥ CULTURE & TRADITION by Lois Pearce, a Master Bridal Consultant™ with extensive knowledge in matters of wedding traditions, heritage and culture.

❤ MUSIC AND DANCE by Jeff Allen, author, choreographer and leading dance consultant. Jeff is the feature writer for *Dancing USA* magazine.

❤ PHOTOGRAPHY by Pat Taylor, a veteran photographer since 1969. At the peak of his wedding photography business, Pat covered over 150 weddings a year, and has photographed well over 1000 weddings in his career.

❤ HONEYMOONS by Jack Benoff, a favored consultant to the travel industry, specializing in honeymoon destinations.

Just when we thought we'd heard it all…there is a section at the end with questions and answers we have received that you might think would never be asked.

Feel free to bend, bookmark and highlight the pages —we want you to USE THIS BOOK!

*P*lanning a wedding is a lot like running a corporation. You have to know a little about many different things to make the proper decisions. You must hire people to provide services for you. Most importantly, you must budget and coordinate the whole event without letting the little details slip away.

Our parent company started as a catering firm looking for an effective way to market that specialized service. In 1989 we published the Michigan Wedding Guide, a wedding directory and guidebook that grew from a local publication to state-wide distribution with multiple guides.

After many years in the wedding business and the growing popularity of the Internet, we realized the need for national access to information about wedding planning. In 1996 our Internet design and marketing company, WD Web.Company (www.wdweb.com), was created to make our wedding guides available on the World Wide Web in the form of Wedding Details. Wedding Details (www.weddingdetails.com) quickly grew to include its sister site, Party Details (www.partydetails.com), and eventually evolved into the comprehensive on-line wedding planning source it is today, serving between fifty and ninety thousand unique users each month, that's over one million actual people each year.

Wedding Details includes a broad list of service providers from all over the United States, as well as honeymoon destination and travel information from all over the world. We have the most complete panel of experts to assist you in everything from wedding day schedule planning, to seating arrangements, to what song should be played for that special "first dance".

Extensive research and professional wedding experts are the backbone of the success of Wedding Details. The vast amount of information on the Wedding Details site...planning, lore and traditions, honeymoons, bridal shows, music and dance, and jewelry...has been thoroughly researched in order to provide the most up-to-date information in the 45 billion dollar wedding industry.

The staff of Wedding Details wishes you the best of luck on your special day and we know that you will find the questions, and answers, in this book helpful as you plan the big event.

Best wishes from the staff at Wedding Details, Inc., and we hope you visit us online soon.

Michael Connors, President   Katherine Karr, COO

Etiquette

by
EDITH GILBERT

PARENTS, STEP-PARENTS, CHILDREN AND
OTHER FAMILY MATTERS

Q. Should I have my father give me away at my wedding when I honesty feel that he did not accept his responsibilities to me as a father, nor did he have much interest in my life. Does he deserve this privilege?

A. I truly understand your feelings toward your father, who it seems has neglected you. So, if you wish, you may walk down the aisle by yourself or with your mother or someone else of your choice. On the other hand, isn't this a good time to overcome bitterness, begin the process of forgiveness and start the rest of your life on a more wholesome and positive path? If you have children your father might turn out to be a good grandfather—this has happened and fences as well as relationships have been mended as time goes by.

Q. We are having a problem trying to decide whether or not to invite my fiancé's stepmother to the wedding. I will be polite in saying that she is not one to bring to any type of social gathering and we do not want this to turn out to be a disaster. We would, however, like to invite my fiancé's father. How do we ask him to attend alone without causing a problem?

A. I am sorry, my dear, but you cannot invite your fiancé's father without his wife. It probably won't turn out as badly as you fear. Can you assign someone to look after her? Good luck!

Q. My fiancé and I are getting married next summer. My parents are divorced and don't really communicate with each other. What do I do about seating arrangements at the ceremony and reception?

A. You can seat parents at the ceremony as follows: mother in the first aisle, father (and spouse?) in second or third aisle. At the reception have two parents' tables reserved with place cards and seat them with close relatives or friends.

Q. We sent out formal wedding invitations to our family and friends and now we are getting calls asking, "Can I bring a date, my children, a visiting aunt..." What can we say in response without offending anyone?

A. To begin with, the name of EACH guest is written on the inside envelope of the wedding invitations, e.g. *Mr. and Mrs. Wilson*. If small children or teen-agers are invited, their first names are written below the parents' names, e.g. *Samantha and Eric, Miss Wilson*. Individual invitations are sent to adults all living under one roof. When single persons are invited, the name followed by the words "and guest" or "and escort" is written on the inside envelope. To answer how to respond to "uninvited guests," I suggest consideration and tact. "We appreciate your inquiring about Aunt Lucy. You know, we've all gone over the guest list very carefully—there are so many friends we wish we could have included, but we are quite limited in space and budget and cannot increase our list. I hope you'll understand our inability to include your *date, friend, child,* etc."

Q. My fiancé has a 15-year old daughter. Do I have to have her in my wedding party? What else can I have her do? I get along fine with her but I want to keep the wedding party small.

A. No, my dear. The 15-year-old does not need to be in your wedding party. She could have the honored role of handing out programs, or be in charge of the guest book, lighting the ceremonial candles or be in charge of receiving wedding gifts. The roles of bridesmaids and groomsmen are usually reserved for siblings or cousins of the bride and groom, not their children.

Q. My fiancé's family is pressuring me to have his one year-old niece and two-year-old nephew in the wedding party. I think

they are too young. How do I handle this without hurting their feelings?

A. Explain to them that you have taken their wishes under serious advisement. Unfortunately, you have been informed that anyone under 6 years of age is not sufficiently dependable and ought not be considered to play a role in the wedding party.

Q. My fiancé would like to include his daughter's name on our invitation. I am not sure if this is right, or how to do it. She will be our flower girl, and will be mentioned in the program. I don't want the invitation to look like a "book."

A. Please tell your fiancé that children age 5 are not hosts and their names do not belong on an invitation. Her role a flower girl is sufficient. You can also offer her the first piece of wedding cake after you each have a bite.

INVITATIONS, THANK-YOU NOTES AND OTHER NECESSARY WORDS

Q. A friend of ours suggested that we mail most of our wedding invitations three to four weeks before the wedding and hold back a bunch to mail after some of the refusals arrive. Would that be O.K.?

A. Sorry, but your friend is off base. ALL wedding invitations are mailed at the same time so that all guests will receive them within the same week. You may figure that on an average, 30% more or less of the invited guest will not be able to attend, especially if it involves out-of-town travel. Even after people have accepted, there are last minute unforeseen circumstances, which force people to regret up to the last day. It would be in poor taste to have invitations arriving to some people a week before the wedding, when others have received them weeks before. Incidentally, invitations should be sent out at least 4-6 weeks before the wedding.

Q. Is it necessary to order announcements—to whom are they sent and when?

A. A wedding announcement is NOT an invitation to a wedding. It does not require a gift and it is mailed the day AFTER the wedding. The announcement says in effect, "I'd like you to know that I am married!" Nothing more—nothing less. Sending an announcement is just another option for the bride and groom to inform friends and family of the news. It is often a good solution when the wedding ceremony is very small, or takes place in another state, or when there is a very small reception or none at all.

Q. My fiancée and I both work, so we are pressed for time. Is it all right for us to divide the thank you notes and each write some?

A. Many couples do this. A few sentences on a small informal foldover are sufficient. The person who writes the note should sign his or her name only though, because only one person can write a note. However, one should always include the other person in the body of the note, "Mary was thrilled when we opened your gift," or "Bill can't wait to try the new coffee maker."

Q. How do you feel about including an e-mail address to RSVP an invitation?

A. Miss Manners may not agree with this, but since people have become even more lax in answering all invitations—any answer, even e-mail, is better than no answer!
In France during the 18th century, guests were fined 5 francs for not responding to an invitation, which was delivered by a footman in livery. Ideally, a response to a written invitation should be a <u>written</u> response, especially to a formal wedding invitation.

Q. We have not received some responses from invited guests. If a response is not received by the requested date, is it appropriate to call the guest and ask if they are attending? We are

having a formal, sit down dinner, and cost per guest is quite high.

A. Absolutely YES! I strongly recommend you call people you have not heard from and ask if they received the invitation; and if so, are they planning to attend?

SHOWERS, PRE-NUPTIAL PARTIES, GIFTS AND OTHER FUN STUFF

Q. I am planning to give my brother and his bride-to-be a wedding shower. It was brought to my attention that it might not be "proper" for a sister to give her brother a shower.

A. Traditionally it is correct for friends, bridesmaids, honor attendants— and not family members—to host a shower because it could appear "grabby" for gifts. However, it would be okay if you offer to co-host a shower with one of the above mentioned people, but let the invitation come from them.

Q. My future in-laws have not offered to host the rehearsal dinner. My parents have offered to pay for the dinner. Should my fiancé and I pay for the dinner? How do I handle the in-laws?

A. It would be best if you step aside and let your fiancé talk to his parents and explain that it is customary for the groom's parents or members of his family to host the rehearsal dinner, but if this is not convenient other arrangements need to be made. In addition, he might add that the rehearsal dinner need not be a formal affair. Casual is quite appropriate.

Q. How can we ask guests to give us money instead of gifts since we are having our wedding in Barbados and it will be expensive to bring home gifts?

A. There is no way you can ask guests for money instead of gifts. Your family or close friends could suggest a monetary gift as an option, if and when they are asked where you are registered. Or, you can register for gifts in the United States and instruct the stores to send the gifts to your home either before you leave or after you return from Barbados.

Q. Close friends of ours are marrying for the second time and they both have complete households filled with lovely things. Do you have any suggestions for an appropriate wedding gift?

A. While browsing on the Internet, I came across this helpful list, courtesy of *Town and Country Magazine.* Dancing lessons, a weekend at a spa, subscription to theater, ballet or opera, a year of flowers, donation to a charity in their names, cooking lessons, consultation with a decorator or garden designer, loan of a vacation house, adopt a tree or bench in a local park in their name.

Q. My daughter just cancelled her wedding three weeks before the ceremony. How do we deal with shower and wedding gifts? Must they all be returned?

A. The gifts should not have been used. I suggest gifts that have not been used should be returned. Those that have been used, your daughter ought to write a sweet note and thank the donor for the gift (AGAIN IF NEED BE) and write that unfortunately the wedding has been called off and she is unable to return the shower gift since she has enjoyed using it so much and is "so appreciative of your love and understanding."

Q. Do you know of any company that provides wedding insurance to cover cancellation of a wedding, or no-show vendors, or losses due to theft or damages? My sister had an unfortunate experience due to a hurricane.

A. Yes, there is a company, "Wedding Insurance" underwritten by the Fireman's Fund. RV Nuccio and Assoc. in Fawnskin, California, 92333 administer it, exclusively. **Telephone 1 (800)-engaged**. They cover a wide variety of reasons for wedding cancellations.

WEDDING CEREMONIES, WEDDING PARTIES, BRIDAL PARTIES, SECOND WEDDINGS, ATTIRE, AND OTHER PARTY PARAPHERNALIA

Q. I think one of my bridesmaids may drop out of the wedding, which is 18 months away. How do I go about asking someone else to replace her without making them feel like I'm asking them to be in the wedding just to fill in a spot?

A. It is way too soon to ask anyone to be your attendant! Too many unforeseen circumstances could arise in 18 months. Six months before the wedding is a good time to ask relatives and friends to participate in your wedding. You can do it then without explanation or apologies.

Q. My ex-husband and I are remarrying. I would like to have ceremony and invite family and friends. We had a big wedding 10 years ago, so how does one word the invitations to a second wedding? How many attendants should we have?

A. If you wish to handle this second wedding tastefully, I suggest you have a private ceremony with your immediate family and a few close friends. (Same for Renewal of Vows). You only need two witnesses, a matron of honor, and a best man. Invitations could simply be handwritten notes inviting to " a private wedding ceremony (renewal)—time, place, date. Please let us know if you will be able to celebrate with us."

Q. We are planning a September wedding and I would like to wear a pretty wedding dress with a short veil. My fiancé does not care to rent a tuxedo. Do you have any suggestions?

A. It is becoming more popular these days for the groom and his attendants not to rent tuxedoes for informal or garden weddings. Instead they may choose to wear navy blazers and matching ties and pants in a color that compliments the bridesmaids' gowns.

Q. My daughter is getting married and her fiancé does not want to choose a best man. He says anyone who happens to be standing by can witness the signing of the marriage certificate. What do you think?

A. The best man has a larger role to play than the groomsmen. In addition to witnessing the signing of the marriage certificate, he hands the ring to the groom during the ceremony; he proposes the first toast at the reception. When duties are assigned, not left to chance, everything will go more smoothly and there will be less chance for mistakes and worry.

Q. Please advise on the toasting ceremony. Who stands, who sits? Who drinks, who doesn't? Who clinks glasses, and when is the best time to propose a toast?

A. In America the following customs usually apply. At a large gathering, the person proposing the toast usually stands. At a small gathering, one merely raises their glass and remains seated. A toast should be light and short. Three minutes is maximum, one minute is often better. Never give an off-color toast or put someone down. The person or couple being toasted remains seated. They may respond with a pleasant "thank you," and a few words of welcome. Guests remain seated and raise their glasses, then take a sip. Clinking of glasses is optional. One theory of clinking the glass is to frighten away evil spirits.

The best time to offer a toast is between courses or before dessert is served. Sometimes a welcoming toast is offered before the main meal.

$\mathscr{M}$other-of-the Bride Matters

by
SHERRI GOODALL

INTRODUCING THE EXALTED M.O.B....

Q. What are the duties of the Mother of the Bride—especially if she lives in Belgium, the bride lives in Orlando, Florida, AND the wedding will be in Toledo, Ohio?

A. The first thing I would do is obtain a wedding planner or someone in the city of the wedding to "run herd" on all those folks providing wedding services. It would be almost impossible to plan your daughter's wedding from a continent away, especially when the bride herself is not in the wedding city!

Q. My daughter asked me to be her Matron of Honor. I am not familiar with this, What is the proper role, Mother of the Bride, or Matron of Honor?

A. I was also asked to be my daughter's Matron of Honor, and it was one of the greatest joys for me to oblige. You can be both. Your duties as the Matron of Honor are to attend your daughter at the altar, raise and lower her veil if necessary, and help her with her bridal gown train. Otherwise, your role as the Mother of the Bride remains to help your daughter plan her wedding and be by her side.

Q. We have determined to give our daughter a set amount of money for her wedding. Our only request is that the wedding and reception take place in the same town where out-of-town guests will be staying, so that no one has to travel during possible bad weather. Our future son-in-law is pushing for a small church an hour out of town—no room for dressing, greeting guests, etc. I don't want to seem like a meddling mother-in-law, but this venue for the wedding seems unworkable. As hosts, don't we have some say-so on this matter? Neither our daughter nor her groom has allegiance to a particular faith at this time. Thanks for your help.

A. I didn't hear anything about how the bride feels. As hosts you definitely have a say-so, but I think your daughter should be a decision-maker as well. Your point of view makes more sense if for no other reason than convenience. And, as a host you do need to consider your guests. You are the M.O.B.; perhaps some gentle, but convincing reason and leadership are necessary here—with the bride's assist. Good luck!

Q. I have seen the bride give her mother a rose or a flower from her bouquet. What is this tradition, and is there a certain color rose that you use?

A. This is a sentimental tradition. The rose or flower should be taken from the bride's bouquet (the florist should see that this bloom is "loose" in the bouquet) and given to the mother at the end of the walk down the aisle. In Medieval times the groom plucked a flower from the bride's bouquet and put it in his buttonhole, thus the "boutonniere"...all the flowers derive from the bride's bouquet.

Q. My future son-in-law wants to be included in such decisions as wedding flowers, menu, and photography. Since my husband and I are taking financial responsibility for the entire wedding and reception, is it proper for the bridegroom to accompany my daughter and me to meeting with the different vendors? Thank you.

A. A lot depends on your relationship with your future son-in-law and his relationship with your daughter. Today's bridal couples are older, savvier, and more opinionated—even though you are the financial contributors. You might discuss it with your daughter, but I would be very careful of alienating either one of them.

You'll learn that some battles are worth fighting for, others are best left alone. Whatever goes on before and during the wedding can upset a whole lifetime...a word to the wise! You want to remain in-laws, not out-laws.

IN-LAWS, OUT-LAWS, PARENTS AND STEPPARENTS... ALL THAT FAMILY!

Q. My question is a very difficult one. My mother passed away a few years ago and my father has just recently remarried. I am engaged to be married soon. My question is how do I address the mother-of-the bride? Do I include my new stepmother? I get along great with her but I feel like I just can't call her mother. How do I address this at the wedding, and in the newspaper announcement?

A. Your first question on "how to address the mother-of-the-bride: Call her by her first name; she is not your mother, nor the mother-of-the bride. In your wedding announcement, you are the daughter of your father e.g. Mr. and Mrs. (your stepmother) John Smith...and the late Beverly Smith (your mother). Note: *in your invitation you do not include name of the deceased as host.*

As long as you have a great relationship with your stepmother, you must treat her with respect. I don't know what you have planned for a processional, so I don't know if she will be included. I assume your father is walking you down the aisle. Beyond that, she should be included as your father's wife.

Q. My daughter just got engaged over the holiday. It is time to meet the young man's parents. Is it up to me to make the arrangements? Should we call and invite them to our home or out to dinner so that we can meet our daughter's future in-laws?

A. In either case, don't stand on ceremony! If you are comfortable with inviting the future in-laws to your home, go ahead and do it. If going out to dinner would be less stressful, then go with that plan. There's no hard and fast rule as to who invites whom first, although the bride's parents seem more often to have the role of "hosts."

Q. My parents have been divorced for 15 years. I love them both, and I want my dad and mom to walk me down the aisle. My mom doesn't think my dad should have that honor. My mom is paying for my wedding. She said she will compromise by letting my dad walk me down the aisle, but only to the second pew where she will then "give me away." I think this is dumb. What do you think? She says she'd rather my grandfather walk me down if she can't do it. HELP!

A.   Sounds like your mom has the answer that might suit everyone...she and your dad walking down the aisle to the second pew and then having her step forward to give you away. Your dad should be allowed a kiss. You have to compromise here, since your mother is paying for the wedding, but your feelings for your dad are important too. In many cultures both parents walk the bride down the aisle.

Q. My daughter is getting married soon and I am already worrying about all the duties and details AFTER the wedding. What should I do?

A.   There is quite a bit to do after the wedding. Perhaps your daughter can designate a "Head Bridesmaid" to help with all the details so you don't have to worry. Some of the things to consider: Transporting wedding gifts home, saving the piece of cake for the bride and groom, collecting and distributing flower arrangements, food, looking for items left in dressing rooms, return of rental tuxedoes, collecting toasting glasses, cake knives, bouquets, etc.

Q. What order does the wedding party come out and where does everyone stand?

A. The traditional order is:

  Grandparents

  Groom's parents

Bride's mother, can be seated in front row to wait for father who escorts bride. After bride reaches altar, mother and father can go up and stand beside her, or father is seated next to mother in front row.

Groomsmen
Bridesmaids (Maid or Matron of Honor last)
Flower girls ring bearers
Bride and father

Groom usually comes out with Best Man and those officiating before processional.

Parents can stand to side of bride and groom (respective parents by their child). Best Man and Maid of Honor also stand by the bride and groom. Attendants can stand in rows on either side of bride and groom, facing outward, but turning towards bride and groom when actual wedding ceremony begins. Attendants can stand as pairs, or all girls, all guys. They walk back down the aisle in pairs…in reverse order of processional.

Q. My fiancé's parents are divorced and his father has been remarried for many years. Everyone gets along great (including his mom and stepmom), but I need to know the correct processional order for mothers and who escorts them.

A. Traditionally the bride and groom's grandparents and parents come down first. In your situation the stepmother would come first with her husband (since they all get along), the groom's mother with an usher or another son. Your mother would come last; also with a son or an usher, assuming your father walks you down the aisle. Then proceed with groomsmen, bridesmaids, flower girl, etc., then you.

THE GUESTS …WHO, HOW AND WHEN?

Q. My daughter is getting married in Las Vegas. I will be giving her a reception/party a month after the wedding at our home, in a different locale. How do we invite guests that

were not invited to the wedding? Is it OK to give her a wedding shower before the wedding? She feels that she can't
have a shower because she is not inviting anyone but immediate family to the wedding.

A. It would <u>not be</u> "socially correct" to entertain your daughter with
a shower (immediate family usually do not give showers) before her
wedding to which only family members are invited. Instead, having a
reception (after the wedding) honoring the newly married couple
would be in fine taste. Many people will bring or send gifts after the
fact.

OKAY, THE DETAILS...WHO PAYS FOR WHAT?

Q. As far as financial obligations, who pays for what

A. Traditionally, the bride's family paid for everything, including a
dowry for the groom (all this just to get her married!). Today, it is a
different story...everything from "shared" expenses where both families contribute equally, bride and groom share expenses, bride pays for
her guests, groom pays for his...or to the groom's parents paying for
liquor, flowers and music. Some bride's families pay for all the reception costs and the groom's families pay for the ceremony flowers,
music, officiant's fees, rehearsal dinner and honeymoon expenses. You
can really decide what fits your budget best.

Q. Our rehearsal dinner will be the first time for many of
our guests to meet. Do you have any suggestions to make
this easier and more fun, rather than stuffy place cards?

A. Assuming your dinner isn't too formal, you can make "fun"
nametags as follows: Use tags with two different color borders (blue
and pink, red and blue, etc.) At the top of the nametags print
"F.O.B." (family/friends of the Bride) use matching pen for names of

her guests, print **"F.O.G."** at the top of the groom's guests (friends/family of the Groom) and use matching pen for his guests. You can use plastic holders with cords that slip around the neck so no need for pins or sticky stuff on clothes. Depending on budget and size of party you can also do buttons, or ball caps or tee shirts. You can also use different color clothes and napkins, but mix your guests so that they can really mingle and meet.

Q. Who is invited to the rehearsal dinner/pre-nuptial party besides the bridal party and parents?

A. Usually out-of-town guests, immediate family, officiants and their spouses, and any close, close friends not in bridal party.

Q. My daughter is being married this summer and has asked me to wear ivory, like her dress. Would it proper for the mother-of-the-groom to wear ivory too?

A. It might be difficult to get all those ivories to be compatible. Perhaps the mother-of-the-groom could coordinate her dress with the bridesmaids' dresses.

Q. My future son-in-law would like a "groom's cake." What exactly is a groom's cake? When is it served?

A. The groom's cake is often chocolate, and more whimsical than the "wedding" cake. It can be shaped in sports themes, autos, body parts (ahem)…anything the groom wants. Often, guests take home pieces of the groom's cake as favors. The story goes that if a single woman puts the cake under her pillow at night, she will dream of her future husband. Whoever bakes the wedding cake can bake a groom's cake. It is served at the same time.

Q. My fiance and I want to elope to have our own private thing without families and then have a big wedding later for

everyone. Our parents are not going to understand our logic on this and will not help with arrangements. We have our license already but I don't know where to go for an officiant. Neither of us belongs to a church. We were thinking of getting a Justice of the Peace but I don't know where to find one. Please help.

A. Try calling the County Clerk's Office for a list of Justices of the Peace.

Q. I am having a hard time trying to buy my fiancé a gift. Any suggestions?

A. Depends on his interests. Sports—logo jerseys, clothes or tickets to a game, outdoors—equipment, jewelry—watches, cuff links, anything monogrammed, collector books, silver photo frames (with your picture), bar ware.

Traditions & Culture

by
LOIS PEARCE

Q. I have a 7-year old brother that I would like to include in our wedding ceremony. I have already chosen a flower girl (four-year-old niece), and I don't really want a ring bearer. My mother suggested having a Jr. Bride and Bridegroom (I also have a 7 year-old cousin that could fulfill the Jr. Bride role). Have you ever heard of this idea in a wedding ceremony?

A. In some Latin American weddings a young girl and young boy are dressed as a miniature bride and groom. The young lady wears a white dress similar to the length and style of the bride's dress. The young gentleman would wear what the groom wears.

Q. What are the requirements from the government of Mexico to be married there if you are not currently a resident?

A. The most accurate information may be obtained from the Consulate or Mexican Embassy office in the Washington D.C.

Q. We are planning on a military (Army) wedding. The problem is, neither my fiancé' nor myself can locate reference material on how, exactly, to conduct a military wedding. The Army does not generate a formal outline for such an occasion. If you have any info or can point me in the right direction, I would appreciate it very much. Thank you.

A. A military wedding is like any other wedding. The ceremony itself is not a military service, but a religious one. What makes it a military wedding is the attire and perhaps some traditions not found in a civilian wedding. The arch of sabers takes place immediately following the ceremony usually on the steps or walk. Weapons are not carried inside the church. It is traditional, as the couple passes through the arch of swords, that the last two members of the arch lower their sabers in front of the couple, detaining them momentarily, while a saber bearer commands: "The price of passage is one kiss". At the same time, another saber bearer on the right, with his saber, gives the bride a gentle "swat" on the rump and utters, "Welcome to the Army." This step is omitted if the bride is in the military. Only commissioned officers generally may participate in the arch.

Q. I was hoping that you would be able to give me some information on the tradition of having a wedding cake and what it symbolizes in American /Irish culture. My fiancé is hesitant to have a cake because he doesn't like it. Would you be able to supply me with such info, I would be more than grateful.

A. The wedding cake is a central point of every wedding reception. I have worked with some couples who have not wanted a traditional large wedding cake, but instead have had a smaller wedding cake for the purpose of pictures included on a table of other desserts. Those guests who would like cake could have it and those who don't could chose something else. (However, the downside is that usually guests load up on the sweets, so be sure to choose small plates for a dessert table.) A traditional Irish cake is a rich fruit cake covered in almond paste and white royal icing. It is not unusual for the cake to be in the shape of a heart, clover and horseshoe-shaped cake. The Irish custom is to keep your top layer for the christening of your first child (although you may chose to have this for your first anniversary).

Q. My fiancé is Jewish (from a pretty conservative family from South Africa) I am Catholic - my parents are Japanese and Irish. What kinds of traditions can we incorporate into our wedding to reflect all of our cultures? We are planning on having a chuppah and we're being married by a reformed rabbi - what suggestions do you have for the Japanese and Irish traditions? Thanks!

A. Japanese traditions include: serving red rice, kelp, fish as reception foods, sake as a beverage. Red is the joyous, lucky color. You may want to tie the napkins in a red ribbon. Since I don't know your color scheme this is only a suggested way of bringing in the color. At a traditional Japanese reception there are many speeches and toasts. Perhaps you may want to select some of your favorite relatives or friends to give toasts throughout your wedding reception. For example, if there is a relative or a close friend of your father's, if you chose to have a father-daughter dance, they may offer a toast or special words just before you take that dance. Usually the Japanese bride changes clothing three times. One dress for the wedding ceremony, one for the beginning of the reception, and then a red dress towards the end. Irish: The couple is showered with flower petals.

Q. As an American woman marrying a British man, what English wedding traditions should I know about?

A. The English bride carries a ribbon-bedecked horseshoe on her arm for good luck. Traditionally she would have only one adult attendant as a witness or to have many young bridesmaids instead of adult attendants. The bride and groom dance a first dance but there is no introduction of the wedding party or a father/daughter dance. They do not toss the bouquet or garter.

Q. My future husband is Indian & his family practices Hinduism. My family is Italian & practices Catholicism. It will be a civil ceremony. We would like to include some small aspects of his Indian heritage to the day, however he doesn't really know any. His mother has a tendency to get carried away. We were hoping you could provide subtle cultural traditions that we could include. The wedding will be small (approx. 30 people). Any sort of cultural information you could provide or refer us to would be extremely helpful!

A. A Hindu ceremony is an elaborate experience. It usually occurs over several days with various different aspects. Prior to the ceremony you may consider having the exotic, intricate patterns decorating your hands and feet with henna. (This is called Mehandi.) It is believed that the deeper the color, the stronger her love for her husband. You may exchange floral garlands as a part of your ceremony or have rose petals strewn over your shoulders after your exchange of vows.

Q. My daughter is planning to be married. She is interested in "Jumping the Broom," (An African Custom). I am interested in obtaining information about how this is accomplished. Are there any tribal customs regarding the formality? Is this simply stated at the end of the pronouncement? Please help.

A. "Jumping the Broom" is most associated with couples who were forbidden from being married during slavery. As their way of "legally" being married at the end of the ceremony they would "jump the broom", as if jumping into matrimony. You must check with the wedding officiant as some will not allow this ceremony to take place during the service since it is not religious in nature. It is held at the conclusion of the ceremony, after the benediction. A straw broom (usually decorated with ribbons and flowers on the broom handle and the top of the broom itself) is placed down in front of the bride and groom, either by the maid of honor and best man or another designated person. The officiant may announce what is about to take place and then the bride and groom jump over the broom together. The broom may also be brought to the altar by dancers and drummers, who, after the couple jumps over the broom may lead then back down the aisle of the church. This same procedure may be held at the reception if not permitted at the ceremony.

Q. Hi Lois, I was just wondering if there are any alternatives to the traditional tossing of the garter and bouquet.

A. A Peruvian custom is to place wedding charms separately on thin ribbons and have the ribbons implanted between the top two layers of the cake. Your single bridesmaids pull the ribbons and the girl who pulls the charm with the ring on it is the next one to be married.

Q. My son is marrying a woman who is from Taiwan and many of her family will be flying to New York for the occasion. Is there anything I should advise people not to do that her family might find offensive.

A. When meeting someone for the first time, a nod of the head is sufficient. Chinese women will rarely shake hands. If you would like to offer them flowers for any reason make sure you give an even number. An odd number of flowers would be very unlucky. If there are any children do not touch the head of another person's child. It is believed they may be damaged by careless touching. Avoid any gifts of cutting tools (knifes, scissors, etc.) it suggests the severing of a friendship. Avoid gifts or wrapping paper where the predominant color is white, black or blue. Elderly people are very highly respected, so it is polite to let them speak first. Acknowledge them first in a group, and do not smoke or wear sunglasses when they are near.

Q. I told my mother that I was getting married in the Bahamas. She stated that marriages in the Bahamas are illegal and are not recognized by the United States. Is this true? and if so what steps do I need to take to get my marriage legally recognized in the state of Virginia.

A. A wedding in the Bahamas is a recognized marriage in the United States if you follow the correct procedures. Contact the Registrar General in Nassau. Their telephone number is 809-322-3316. You may also contact the Ministry of Tourism 809-328-7810 for information. No blood test is necessary. The fee for the license is $40.00. Some brides chose to go to their town hall and have a civil ceremony just to insure it will all work out and then have a wedding with all the trimmings at the destination of their choice.

Q. My fiancé and I have a "wonderful" problem. We have 9 people (on each side) who mean the world to us, and who we want to stand with us on our wedding day. They include family and friends, and will all be asked because we love them, not because we feel we HAVE to ask them. The problem comes with the maid of honor/best man. We each have three people who without their love and support, we would have never become the people who we are, the person that the other loves. Each of the three (for both my groom and I) have played

a different, yet important role in our lives. Two of the three (on each side) are friends, the third being a sibling. We are having an incredibly difficult time choosing who should fill those special roles. We could choose family and avoid hurting anyone, but we truly want the others to have the special title and place in our ceremony, too. I have seen a maid and matron of honor, and two best men at other weddings, but would three be too extreme? I know this is our wedding, but we don't want people to judge us for having so many best men and maids/matrons of honor. We also don't want the three to feel slighted by sharing the role with two others, or for the remaining 6 attendants to feel they aren't even among the top 3 of our closest friends. We feel we have to go with either one or three, as two would just leave someone out. We have been engaged for almost two months, and are anxious to ask our bridal party, but we can't make this difficult decision! Help! Any opinions or ideas on how best to handle this situation?

A. Part of the wedding planning process is making hard decisions and not offending anyone. Certainly your friends, if they are really your friends, should not be offended if you ask your siblings to serve as either your maid/matron of honor and best man. Each of the persons could be given an important duty instead of giving any one all of them. There are several ways to accomplish this. If you are looking to distinguish them by clothing and flowers, the three ladies could wear the same dress color or they could have bouquets, which are different from the other attendants. One could hold your flowers during the ceremony, one could lift your veil, and one could be responsible for making sure your train is nicely adjusted during the ceremony. You could also have your sibling as your honor attendant and the other two could be in the bridal party and during the ceremony they each have a reading. For the gentlemen, one could escort your mother, one the groom's mother and one serve as the best man to hold the rings. The gentlemen as well could be distinguished by different lapel boutonnières. Each of your honored persons could offer at toast at some time during the reception, there are no rules on the number of toasts offered.

Q. I am Jewish, my fiancé is Hindu. We are getting married on a Saturday morning (a big no, no in the Jewish faith), so there is no rabbi who will marry us. We want to deputize my great uncle so that he will perform our ceremony in August 2001. I can't seem to find out how to get him deputized for the day in California (he lives in Maryland). Can you help? Thanks.

A. Contact the County Clerk's office in the town where the wedding will take place. They will inform you if this is possible.

Q. When is the right time to get remarried? I have been married for ten years. Is now the right time to renew our vows?

A. There is no right or wrong time to renew your vows. Many couples will usually do so on a landmark anniversary, 1, 5, 10, 15, etc.

Q. This isn't a culture question but I want to ask you anyway! If I have a child from a previous relationship and she accepts him as her daddy and vice versa how can we include her in the wedding as though we are all joining our lives together?

A. There is a jewelry item called the Family Medallion, which could be presented to her during your wedding ceremony by your fiancé. The officiant may offer a prayer and make this a special moment. Contact Clergy Services (800-237-1922) for information.

Q. How can I find out if someone is allowed by law to perform wedding ceremonies? A friend of my fiancé's and mine is an ordained minister; I want to know if he can legally marry us.

A. Contact your local county clerk's office. They will be able to provide you with the most accurate information. Usually, once you obtain your marriage license from the clerk's office you are partially married. The officiant only needs to witness the commitment. It varies from state to state and it is important information for you to know about your local rules.

Q. Hi, I am concerned about the role of the participants in my wedding. Latinos have a maid of Honor and a godmother of the wedding, and we have a best man and a godfather of the wedding what are their roles?

A. Usually the godparents "Madrino and Padrino" bring the gifts to the altar. (Lasso, coins, gift to the Virgin Mary, Bible, Rosary.)

Q. I read your information on Eastern Orthodox weddings on the Weddingdetail.com website. I am looking for more information on Russian Orthodox weddings. I would appreciate your assistance. We are hoping to at least do the crowning ceremony, but I need the detail, not just the general description.

A. The priest holds the stephana, (which are two "crowns" - floral wreaths), which are joined by a ribbon. He makes the sign of the cross three times over the bride and groom. The crowning is a sign of victory, as athletes were crowned in ancient times at their triumphs; now, the bride and groom are crowned as mature Christians, prepared for the responsibilities of Christian marriage.

Q. We are also looking for information on a Japanese Sake ceremony called San-san-kudo. I would appreciate any help you can give me.

A. The San-san-kudo is a sharing of sake. The bride and groom drink from three sake cups, which have been stacked one on top of the other, taking three sips from each cup. The groom usually takes the first three sips from the first cup, then the bride is offered the same cup and she also takes three sips. They follow the same procedure with the next two cups. Sake is then shared with the groom's father, groom's mother, bride's father, and bride's mother.

Q. I have heard of the ritual of the salt, what is it?

A. There are two containers of salt (possibly colored). One is for the bride and the other symbolizing the groom. The pastor reads the passage in Gen. 2 (I think) about how "for this reason a man shall leave his father and mother and shall cleave to his wife and the two shall become one flesh." Then either the pastor or the couple pours the two containers into a third one. The pastor challenges the couple to let this salt be easier to separate than the bond that has been made between these two.

Q. I need to know what order the reception usually goes in. Do we cut the cake first or what? I am not sure so I need some help. If you could just let me know the usual order of things I would really appreciate it.

A. Many facilities will suggest a different format for the wedding reception so that many of the ceremonial aspects take place while they are handling the food service. One example of a formal order for a wedding reception is as follows: Introductions: Brides parents, Groom's parents, Bridal Party, Maid of Honor/Best Man, Flower Girl, Ring Bearer, Bride and Groom. Best Man offers toast. Bridal couple can have their first dance before dinner is served, or wait until after dinner. Parent dances with the bride and groom. After dinner the cutting of the wedding cake (bride feeds groom piece of cake first, followed by groom feeding bride). Bouquet and garter toss are usually the final activities to take place unless there are other ethnic or cultural celebrations.

Q. We are having a small wedding out of town and my parents are hosting a reception for us in our hometown two weeks later. When should my mother send the reception invitations?

A. The reception invitations would be mailed at the same time the wedding invitations would be mailed, usually six to eight weeks before the wedding.

Q. Do you have the ceremony for the tasting of spices? I am getting married in Texas, and have not been able to find an Afro centric person. We are having a pretty traditional Catholic ceremony but I would love to have this take place.

A. Afoshe is the ceremony of tasting of five spices. The groom tastes first, then the bride, then it is passed to the parents, family and other attendees as a sign of ties one to another. The kola nut (1) is first. (In Egypt is used to call upon the spirits. It is a symbol of bitterness that can bring life.) Water (2) represents the abundance of life and the blessings of life. The taste of Honey (3) helps the sweetness in your marriage continue to spread. Pepper (4) is the spice for all life. Salt (5) is an all purpose spice. African ancestors were enslaved because of the pursuit of salt. May it preserve all that is good in your marriage.

Q. First, my fiancé, and I would like to incorporate some traditions from our heritage into our ceremony or reception. He is mostly of German descent, and I have Scottish, Irish, and Yugoslavian ancestors. Any ideas?

A. Scottish: A wedding custom is to have the groom give the bride a silver wedding spoon with the couple's initials engraved on it as a gift. A rich dark fruitcake is served for dessert. The wedding cake is decorated with silver bells and flowers. The top layer is reserved for the christening of the first child. The bride pays for the reception and the groom pays for the flowers and alcoholic beverages.

Irish: The couple exchange claddagh wedding rings (2 hands grasping and a crowned heart to show their love). Single women sign their names under the hem of the brides wedding dress. This is so they will have luck in finding husbands themselves.

Q. Both my fiancé and my brother (who is getting married next year) have mentioned the 'tradition' of shoving the cake into each other's face after cutting it. Can you help my future sister-in-law and I prove to the gentlemen that there is no such 'tradition'? My fiancé was convinced by my 'it's disrespectful and messy' argument (I THINK!?!), but my brother needs more convincing (he's been at friend's weddings where it has taken place).

A. The ceremony of feeding the cake to each other is a sign of how you will respect each other during your married life. If this is so announced by your bandleader or DJ you will receive the respect of your guests not to encourage either party to shove cake to either party.

"Shall we dance?"

*M*usic & Dance

by
JEFF ALLEN

BEFORE THE WEDDING DAY...

Q. Should my fiancé and I take dance lessons for our particular dance? Part of me really wants to look good for our only spotlight dance, but another part of me is nervous and wonders if it would look like too much and too silly?

A. Not at all, you will be dressed to the nines and the stage will be set at the beautifully adorned reception for your memorable moment in the spotlight. You have selected a song that probably means a great deal to both of you. The care you have taken with your dance apart from the ceremony itself reflects time you and your groom have spent together. The first dance historically consummates the wedding vows. The bride says I DO again, in accepting this dance for the rest of her life. So, take lessons and feel comfortable.

Q. If we want to take dancing lessons before the wedding, when should we start?

A. My recommendation is no less than six months in advance. I recommend that any couple that is embarking on such a serious relationship take dance lessons well in advance of becoming engaged or tying the knot. Learning to dance successfully with another is very revealing. A successful dance couple requires cooperation, commitment, patience, and forgiveness. Therefore, learning to dance together becomes a great life skill.

Q. I HATE DANCING! Is there any hope for me? I am getting married and my fiancé loves to dance.

A. A lot of people think they hate dancing. Some do not know how to dance. Some have had a bad experience while dancing in the past. The left side of their brain tells them they need to know how to dance, but their ego may be telling them they're going to look like a fool. This is particularly true in men who are generally left-brain dominant. In all the scenarios, knowledge is the key: LEARN to dance and keep it simple. Knowledge always replaces fear and you will be with someone you love. May I suggest my video or books to help you in the privacy of your home?

Q. How do you slow dance?

A. Slow dancing takes on many forms! It occurs when the music is less than 26 bars of music per minute and should NOT be confused with a fox trot or a waltz. For the non-dancers, they rock together like two monkeys huddled together in the rain. It's a shame when adults still dance like they're in Jr. High School, although they don't look as good - they've grown bigger, and the rear view is not attractive in the older expanded model! We use a two beat increment with a rhythmic hesitating pulse action with a compact ballroom dance position. You can see 15 variations of this on my 2-hour video called - "The Complete Guide to Slow Dancing (www.QuickstartBooks.com)!"

Q. We have taken some lessons but never find the hour or two we need to practice. What should we do?

A. You must be willing to practice often but in short increments of only five minutes. Do it spontaneously! Also, NEVER make your First Dance at the wedding the first time you are dancing in public. You must get out on a social dance floor and "swim with the sharks."

AT THE RECEPTION... THE FIRST DANCE...

Q. When should the Bride & groom dance their first dance and why?

A. First and most importantly conduct the Bride & Groom's dance immediately after their announcement into the reception hall from the receiving line and before dinner! It is correct etiquette for the King & Queen (bride & groom) to open the dance floor. Your DJ or orchestra can play dance music all night long rather than sleepy elevator music. Your guests will have a better time for a longer period. It is common for the older guests to leave earlier in the evening. They miss the opportunity to "cut a rug'" when the wedding dance scenario is left for after dinner. The music and its tempo should become more youthful as the evening continues leaving the opportunity for all to have a great time dancing or simply watching those who can.

Q. What are the room or dance floor preparations that should be made just before the Bride & Goom's First Dance?

A. Have the service people avoid the dance floor while bringing food to the table. If this is not possible because of size limitations, it is a good idea to have the DJ play softer music during the bulk of the main course service time. Spills and accidents happen with drinking, eating, or being served on the dance floor so please be careful that the dancers will not slip and fall. An announcement should be made about five minutes before the entrance is made to clear the dance floor and passageway for the wedding couple. This will also give those guests with cameras an opportunity to get ready. Under no circumstances should anyone, with the possible exception of the photographer, be allowed to cross the dance floor when the Wedding Couple's first dance is taking place or any of the relatives or wedding party's dance takes place.

Q. How much time should the dances that occur in the wedding dance scenario last?

A. Bride & groom's, parent's, mom & dad's, etc... it is not necessary to dance to the whole musical composition. Professional Ballroom & Latin dancers, like myself, doing a show select or edit a composition of no longer than 2 - 2 1/2 minutes per dance. Two minutes for beginners out on the floor by themselves will seem like an eternity! Remember the longer you are out there the more can go awry and you can actually lose the moment. For instance, the father/daughter dance has featured the song *Butterfly Kisses* that last almost six minutes. Only the last two minutes or so of the song deal with the wedding day.

THE FATHER AND DAUGHTER DANCE...

Q. When would be the most effective moment at the wedding reception for the father of the bride and his daughter to dance?

A. I have thoroughly enjoyed the receptions that I have attended including that of my own daughter when the bride and groom danced before dinner and the father/ daughter dance occurred after the cake cutting. The groom danced with his mom immediately following the father/daughter dance. This seemed to me to give each of these three dances their important moment. A general invitation was then given to all of the wedding party and immediate family to dance. There were several opportunities given to change partners and all had a great time without the added pressure on those who did not dance well. Also, this was quick so that the real party could begin!

Q. Do I choose the music for the Father/Daughter dance, or do I give my father the honor? It seems that most of the songs are coming from the father's perspective, so it might be fitting that they get to choose.

A. Most brides should ask this very wise question! Your dad had the honor of presenting you at the ceremony first, and then he has the honor of dancing with you. As for the selection of music, the two of you should discuss this. The lyrics should be based on your relationship and mutual feelings and your abilities to actually dance. Many dads take dance lessons with their daughters as well as their wives. Questions should include; do either of you fox trot or waltz? Do you know that if you choose a slow ballad as a rhythm the slower the tempo the harder it makes the dance? Reputable studios will let the parents share lessons along with the bride & groom.

Q. I have both a father and a stepfather and both are very dear to me. During the wedding ceremony, they are both walking

me down the aisle. During the reception, do I dance with both to separate songs or do I only dance with my biological father? I do not want to offend or hurt either of them.

A. This is a great question. Communication here is very important! The simple answer is: whomever is escorting you down the aisle. However in this case both are (it must be a very wide aisle—make sure three-wide will work). Each man has his feelings about you and the honor of the first dance itself. They can actually share this first dance. Approach each dad to see who would like to start the first dance; the other dad can cut in. This will make them both feel important. At the very least they will both know that you are thinking of their feelings at this time.

Q. I will be escorting my daughter down the aisle and giving her away. Her father passed away and he was the ONLY other male that could have had a special dance with her. She is so upset that it will appear that no one cares about her to the new family. The groom's dance with his mother will just make it more obvious. The two of us have come through so much together but two women dancing together (as some have suggested) just does not seem appropriate. I do not want it turned into something humorous (also what others have suggested).

A. I was very touched by your question. There are many queries like this and each requires an answer with compassion. I do agree that although it happens, I have never felt comfortable recommending that the bride dances with another female family member. I will never tell them not to do it but I do not believe there will be broad -based acceptance by those present at the reception. At this time, a gesture of welcome to the family can be made by the groom's dad. The wedding couple's dance should be conducted at the same traditional time. The groom's father can cut in and dance with the bride, while the groom dances with his mother first, and then the bride's mother. This will certainly be both touching and bonding. This dance moment will be well received by the groom's family and guests. The knot will have been tied at the ceremony so she will in fact, have a new father-in-law. It is an honor to dance with the bride at this time and the groom's dad will probably feel privileged to do so.

THE MOTHER / SON DANCE...

Q. My fiancé lost his mother some time ago so would it be appropriate for him to dance with my mom?

A. It would be perfectly appropriate for your fiancé to dance with your mother or any other woman that he feels has contributed to his life in a very meaningful way. Other choices might be a grandmother, stepmother, aunt, or sister.

Q. We both have parents and stepparents. Is it appropriate to cut in to the mother/son dance to announce a stepmother? Alternatively, should we pick one neutral song that can be used for both stepparents after the father and mother dances are completed?

A. Of your two suggestions, I like the second choice. I am not generally in favor of increasing the number of dances, it tends to lengthen the reception for those watching. Add these dances only if those involved would be offended if they were omitted. As an alternative, you may announce them along with the members of the wedding party and have one big, "wedding party dance."

THE MUSIC LISTS & MUSIC RECOMMENDATIONS:

Q. Where can I find a comprehensive list of First Dance songs as well as all the other musical selections for the other parents' dances and traditions at the reception?

A. You will find "The Wedding Dance Music List ©," at my website: **www.QuickstartBooks.com.** There are over 800 selections in all of the important music and dance categories. Another feature is the listing of the dance type and tempo of each song!

Q. Would you please list some great Fox Trots for our First Dance?

A. *Crazy Love* - Van Morrison, *I Get A Kick Out of You* - Frank Sinatra, *I Love You* - Frank Sinatra, *I Love You More and More Everyday* - Al Martino, *It Had To Be You* – Harry Connick Jr., *L-O-V-E* - Nat King Cole, - Natalie Cole, *Love Is Here To Stay* - Frank Sinatra, *Love of a Lifetime* - Firehouse, *Make Someone Happy* - Jimmy Durante, *Night and Day* - Frank Sinatra, *Only You* - The Platters, Johnny Mathis or Nat King Cole or Natalie Cole, *Too Marvelous For Words* - Frank Sinatra, *Wonderful, Wonderful* - Johnny Mathis, *You Make Me Feel So Young* - Frank Sinatra, *You're Nobody 'Til Somebody Loves You* - Dean Martin.

Q. Would you please list some great waltzes for our First Dance?

A. *Between Now And Forever* - Bryan White, Anne Murray, *Fascination* - Jane Morgan, *Give Me Forever (I Do)* - John Tesh w/ James Ingram, *Kiss From A Rose* – Seal, *Let Me Call You Sweetheart* -Lawrence Welk, *My Cup Runneth Over With Love* - Ed Ames, *Open Arms* – Journey, *So This Is Love "Cinderella"* - James Ingram, *Take it to the Limit* – Eagles, - Forester Sisters, *The Sweetheart Tree* - Johnny Mathis, *Three Times A Lady* – Commodores, *True Love* - Bing Crosby & Grace Kelly, *When I Need You* - Leo Sayer, *With You I'm Born Again* - Billy Preston & Serita, *You Light Up My Life* - Debbie Boone, *You Make Me Feel Like A Natural Woman* Aretha Franklin or Mary J. Blige

CAKE CUTTING...

Q. I wanted to know if you have any suggestions for music to be played while cutting the cake. I <u>hate</u> *The Bride Cuts the Cake* and all my friends have used *When I am Sixty-Four* by the Beatles.

A. How about *Love and Marriage* by Frank Sinatra ? or *Eat It* by Weird Al Yankovic? Or *Who Stole The Keeshka?* ...Frankie Yankovic & His Yanks?

GARTER TOSS AND DOLLAR DANCE...

Q. My fiancé and I have decided to forgo the traditional garter and bouquet tosses at our reception...instead we would like to have a special dance for all of the married couples at our reception, with the longest-married couple receiving a bouquet. Do you have any musical suggestions for this event?

A. Congratulations on what I think is a wonderful idea! It's a celebration of success, I love it!
　　Here are my suggestions for that dance:
　　That's What Friends Are For Dionne Warwick - Fox trot
　　Shower The People James Taylor - Rumba
　　Stand By Me Ben E. King - Rumba
　　We Are Family Sister Sledge - Hustle, West Coast Swing, or Freestyle

Q. Is there some other "tradition" that could be done instead of the "Dollar Dance" at the reception? I'm not terribly crazy about the idea of it.

A. I agree, I think it is tasteless. Many times this dance takes on a rowdy carnival or even a striptease atmosphere. The bride becomes the amusement of the young men and the older ones that haven't grown up. This so-called tradition was born out of a Philippine custom where the "dollar dance" was used by poverty stricken villages to help defray the cost of the wedding and give a little something to the bride & groom to start their new life together. This was the extent of the gift giving and the dance was one of island tradition that said, "thank-you!" Your guests have either presented you with engagement gifts, wedding gifts, or both, therefore many are offended by being asked to give again. Sometimes it becomes a competition - who can pin the most on the donkey - oops I meant the bride. Just forget about it!

UNITY CANDLE...

Q. I'm looking for a song, other than *Wind Beneath My Wings* for our mothers to light the unity candle. My fiancé and I are very close to our mothers and would like a really special song.

A. *One Hand, One Heart* from West Side Story, *The Wedding Song (There Is Love)* Paul Stookey, *Candle On the Water* from the movie 'Pete's Dragon,' *I Love You Forever (I Do)*-James Ingram and John Tesh

THE DJ OR BAND...

Q. Is the DJ also the MC? What questions should I ask when interviewing a DJ or band?

A. Depending on the venue where their host may do this for you or your wedding planner if you have one, the DJ (or BandLeader) may be the best bet for an MC. Ask to see an audition video so you can see their layout as well as hear their voice. Ask to see their play list, their prices—how much $$ for how long, and a list of recent references that you will actually be able to contact!

MULTI-CULTURAL MUSIC ETIQUETTE...

Q. What do I do regarding the mixing of the various ethnic cultures represented at our wedding for the dancing and music?

A. Take a survey from the two representative cultures at your wedding to establish what important musical songs should be played and then make sure at least three from each is played. It is generally fun when those songs are played in succession. The impact is great and each culture can enjoy each other's dancing and or singing especially when a traditional folk dance is done. Since it is nearly impossible for a live orchestra or band to be proficient in two cultures, a DJ is your best bet for the music. In that way, you can provide your guests with the very best versions of each song provided rather than having a live group muddle through something.

WHEELCHAIR DANCING...

Q. I am predominantly wheelchair bound is there any help you can give me for our First Dance?

A. There are many handicapped men and woman that dance in wheelchairs regularly. Once you see how easy and enjoyable this is you'll dance on a regular basis.

I'm going to give you your first lesson in Wheelchair Dancing Basics. You will need to select either a slow ballad or waltz. A slow ballad is written in 4/4 time or waltz in 3/4 time. I will give you three basic steps that are done with your Bride-to-be. The first is the Stride & Glide: This is done by either one or two progressive steps in a forward or backward direction. It is done with a handshake hold either right-to-right or left-to-left in open facing position—partner outside to the left or right (or both) which ever is more comfortable. When used with a slow ballad the step occurs on the second & fourth beat of music and on only the first with a waltz. When your fiancée' is not moving she will close her free foot without weight to the supporting foot. This figure may rotate as much as a quarter of a turn before it is repeated. The second is the Rock & Roll: This figure uses the same timing as above and starts close together either right or left outside partner and is comprised as a rock apart from each other and a roll in together. You can also lead your partner to the third figure called Rope Spinning where you lead her, in the same rhythm, around you like a cowboy with his lasso. A hand change can be used if necessary. During any of these figures, you must use your free hand to keep the timing and the proportion of your movement with the coincidental wheel. It is important that your handholds are comfortable yet firm. Rather than the normal handshake grip, use an interlocking grip with the thumbs facing upwards. Some couples also interlock at the wrists for more security. The consistency of this dance hold and your timing will keep the linear movements accurate!

"Smile..."

All About Photography

by
PAT TAYLOR

Q. Our wedding budget is getting very tight, as everything seems to cost more than we expected. We are trying to cut corners and a friend has offered to take our wedding pictures for free. Would this be a practical alternative for us?

A. When the ceremony is over, all the guests have gone, the flowers have wilted and the DJ has packed up, the only tangible memories you will have of your wedding are the portraits. This is likely one of the most important days of your lives and one you will want to cherish for years to come. Wedding portraits become family heirlooms intended to be passed on for generations. Trusting this critical and permanent element of your special day to a relative or friend, even though they are a real "photo enthusiast", will likely end in disappointment. There is so much more than just "taking pictures" at a wedding. Posing, composition and the complicated lighting challenges of churches can only be handled by proven professional photographers with years of experience. Invite your family and friends to take pictures, but retain a professional photographer to create your wedding portraits. You'll be glad you did.

Q. When should I contract with a photographer for my wedding?

A. The sooner the better. In large metropolitan markets, the better photographers will be booked eighteen months in advance. Often times in smaller towns, bridal couples may wait until approximately nine months to a year before the wedding date. Bridal shows are normally held in January or February to showcase services you might need for your wedding day. Waiting until after these show dates will likely mean the photographer you wish to retain may already be committed. Plan as far ahead as possible.

Q. When interviewing perspective photographers, what should we look for?

A. Any experienced photographer should offer for your inspection a wide variety of wedding samples and albums. These samples should contain not only samples from many different weddings, but they should also include a "complete album" from one wedding. It is easy to pull one or two good samples from many different weddings to display. However, a sample album from one entire event will better help you understand the photographer's style and allow you to accurately evaluate their workmanship.

Q. How can we determine what is truly the "BEST DEAL" when shopping for a photographer?

A. First of all "shopping" for a photographer is very important. I encourage all my bridal couples, with whom I do not have an ongoing professional relationship, to make sure they are entirely comfortable with the photographer they choose. Because of the wide variety of pricing practices employed by different photographers, it can be challenging to come up with an accurate final cost and a full understanding of what that cost includes. Be prepared during the interview to ask a lot of questions.

Some photographers charge by the hour for coverage or by the number of photos taken. Both will likely have limits. Others may offer all inclusive packages which might include everything from the engagement photos to bridal and parents albums. It is extremely important to understand exactly what it is you are paying for. Have the photographer detail the length of coverage they will provide and the entire scope of that coverage. Ask about quantity limits that apply to specific items such as previews, albums or other enlargements. To be a smart shopper you need to know all the facts.

Q. Should I be concerned about a photography studio who subcontracts their weddings to part time photographers?

A. Most large studios that specialize in wedding photography hire part timers to cover the many different weddings they contract for each week. That has been an acceptable professional practice for years. It is likely that the vast majority of wedding photographers nationwide do so on a part time basis and most do a very professional job. However, you do have a right to know who will be showing up to take pictures on your wedding day. The last thing you need in the midst of the wedding day chaos is a total stranger walking up and introducing himself or herself as "Your Photographer". When booking your wedding ask who the photographer will be and request to see some of their workmanship. Try to meet with them prior to the wedding day so you both understand the plan of action for the big day. Be sure that whomever shows up they fully understand what you are expecting from them. Take nothing for granted.

Q. We have heard so much about digital photography and wonder if there are advantages to digital over traditional film and negatives?

A. The photographic profession has witnessed revolutionary changes in just the last two years in the area of digital photography. However, many traditional film photographers, because of the ever-changing technology in the industry and continual improvements in digital capture techniques, are waiting to make the very costly change over. In side by side quality comparisons, you will find little or no difference between the two. Both methods have distinct advantages and limitations. I want to qualify that by saying digital cameras designed for the professional are in the $3,000 to $20,000 price range. These high quality digital cameras create large data files to record your wedding portraits. There is no digital camera on the market priced below those figures, which will allow a photographer to adequately capture your wedding images and be able to produce quality enlargements for you. Ask your photographer what medium he will be using to create your wedding portraits and also inquire as to the type of equipment he will be using.

Q. When should we have engagement portraits taken and published in the newspaper?

A. Again, the time factors depend on your location. Larger metropolitan areas usually have deadlines based on the wedding date for publishing your announcements. Smaller town publications may have much less restrictive time restraints. Check with your local papers and inquire as to their policies.

Many have specific forms which they will require you to complete. Your professional photographer should be able to assist you in preparing to publish your engagement photo.

Q. Traditional wedding photography versus journalistic photography...what's the difference?

A. One of the latest trends in wedding photography is the journalistic style, which is a much less formal approach to capturing your wedding day. Where traditional, as the name implies, offers the more standard form of photography, posed groups, head and shoulder portraits and more controlled photographic atmosphere, journalistic is much more relaxed. More of an "as it happens" format would best describe the journalistic style. The journalistic photographer may shoot black and white or color film, or possibly a combination of both. Many traditional photographers are now offering a mixture of the two styles. Remember a wedding is a family event and while the bridal couple may choose the less formal journalistic style, many parents and grandparents will want the more traditional approach. Try to find a photographer who will strike a balance and meet all the family's needs.

Q. One photographer talked about proofs and another mentioned originals, what's the difference?

A. Proofs, previews, originals, miniature portraits, along with a variety of other labels are affixed to the pictures you receive from the photographer in order to select the enlargements for your albums. These photos can come in a variety of sizes and media. Most are provided in an album for you to review and mark which poses you wish to order, on the accompanying order form. Other photographers project your previews on a screen in their studio and require viewing your wedding portraits there. Some digital photographers may project previews right at the reception. With the advent of the web, more and more photographers are uploading portraits to a host site where you, your family and friends can all visit to view and order your finished albums and photographs. Then there is the photographer who provides no previews at all but instead creates finished albums from the poses they select to go into your album. Again, the options are near limitless and you need to know up front which method your photographer will employ for your wedding.

Q. One photographer stated they wanted us ready three hours before the wedding and another said they only needed an hour. Why such a difference?

A. Styles and personal preference! Some photographers who require extended time prior to the ceremony wish to complete all of the formal group pictures in advance, including those with the bride and groom together. This means immediate family members and the bridal party need to be dressed and ready to go very early. This saves time after the ceremony and allows the bridal party and families generally to get to the reception sooner.

Then there are photographers who segregate the bride and groom before the ceremony photographing them only separately. They save the large formal groups and bride and groom poses until afterwards. This takes more time after the ceremony and will delay the arrival the wedding principals to the reception. For couples who wish to maintain the tradition of not seeing each other before that fateful walk down the aisle, this method assures separation.
An experienced photographer taking bridal couple poses and the formal and family groups after the ceremony can normally complete those shots in less than an hour.

Remember that invited guests are anxiously awaiting the arrival of the wedding party at the reception. Any prolonged delay in the arrival of the party can adversely impact not only these guests but the caterer as well. Determining the time needed for photographs after the wedding should play an integral part in planning a schedule for reception activities.

If you want outdoor portraits taken, you will need to allow for extra time either before or after the wedding. Discuss this in detail with your photographer.

Q. How long after the wedding should we expect to see a selection of our wedding portraits and once ordered, how long should our finished albums take to create?

A. Most photographers should provide your previews within ten to fourteen days after the wedding. Those who project your previews should be willing to set up an appointment for you and your family within the same time frame. The photographer who provides you with a finished album and no originals to review will generally require three to four weeks. When submitting your previews for duplication into final wedding portrait orders it can take up to eight weeks to produce your finished albums.

Q. How long should I be able to keep my wedding previews before placing my order?

A. The time limit varies significantly with each photographer. Many require your originals to be returned with ten days. Others will allow you to keep them a month. While yet others will offer no definite time limit. The belief of the photographers who limit this time is to make sure your order is placed while the excitement of the wedding is still fresh in everyone's mind. However, if your family and friends are spread throughout the country or the world, ten days and even a month may not be enough time. Determine what the ordering deadlines are from your photographer in advance. Make sure they are compatible with your family's needs. If there are family gatherings approaching such as Thanksgiving, Christmas or Easter, try to arrange to keep your previews over that time period to share with family and friends.

Q. How long after the wedding will we still be able to order reprints and enlargements?

A. Ask the photographer how long they retain their wedding negatives or data files. Not only may you wish to reorder portraits at a later date, but accidents can and do happen. Albums can be damaged or destroyed in a variety of ways. Your dog may have never eaten your homework, but I have had them eat wedding albums—must be the leather. Storage is always a concern for photographers and occasionally discarding older files is necessary. Inquire not only how long the photographer will keep your negatives, but also what will they do when it's time to dispose of them. Will they offer you an opportunity to purchase them?

*"How about the
honeymoon, honey?"*

Honeymoons

by
JACK BENOFF

Q. Where are most honeymooners going on their honeymoon?

A. In 2000 some of the most popular places were, Jamaica, Bermuda, Hawaii, Florida, and Italy.

Q. Should I use my maiden name instead of married name on my travel documents?

A. You should use your maiden name on all travel documents. It is highly unlikely that when you travel for your honeymoon that you would have your passport issued with your married name or that you would have had your driver's license re-issued with your married name. When traveling out of the US, it is an excellent idea to have all documents matching.

Q. We have heard about all-inclusive resorts, why or why not should we choose one?

A. If you are someone that likes to do, eat and drink then you should definitely choose an all-inclusive resort. If you are someone that wants to sit on the beach and have a light breakfast, skip lunch and light dinner then you should probably choose a non all-inclusive hotel. The all-inclusive concept truly allows you not to have to keep dipping in your pocket during your honeymoon or get sticker shock on checking out of your hotel. There are some limitations to the all-inclusive concept so research the various resort options and make sure that the one you choose meets your needs.

Q. How do I pick an all-inclusive resort?

A. There are many resorts that call themselves all-inclusive. All-inclusive resorts are primarily located in the Caribbean, Bahamas and Mexico. Their prices are varied, as are the services they provide. For honeymoons look at resorts such as Sandals and SuperClubs. Between these two chains you can find resorts in Jamaica, Bahamas, St. Lucia, and Antigua. Both of these companies offer all beverages (alcoholic and non), meals and snacks in between, entertainment, tips, service charges, watersports and other activities within their packages. Most of their resorts offer 3-5 different restaurants and 3-5 bars, scuba diving, water-skiing and golf included within the package price. Some of the resorts offer room service, in room bars, manicures, dry cleaning, and spas also included within the price. One of the benefits of Sandals is they only allow couples, so you are likely to find many others on their honeymoon.

Q. We are thinking of going on a cruise because we have heard they are "all inclusive." Is that true?

A. The simple answer is NO. While cruises do include the cost of the ship and your meals and entertainment they do not include other items. Typically prior to your cruise the cruise line will ask you for a credit card imprint to put all your shipboard charges on. During the course of a normal cruise you should expect to be charged for tours in the various ports you stop in, drinks while on deck as well as in the dining room (alcoholic and non), activities on the ship, tips to various ship personnel and money spent shopping at the various ports. It is very common for a couple to spend 50% of the amount they spend to book the cruise once they are actually on the cruise. For example if you spend $2000.00 per couple for your cruise it would be common for you to spend $1000.00 during the cruise. If you are truly interested in a honeymoon where you do not have to spend any other money you should look at a resort such as Sandals or SuperClubs.

Q. What is the best way to book my honeymoon?

A. The best way is to use a professional travel agent that has a lot of knowledge about the area and possibly the resort that you want to go to. The Internet is a great place to start searching for information. Before you call a travel agent do as much research as you can to educate yourself. Get as many brochures as you can. When you do choose a travel agent ask if they have been to your specific resort of interest.

Q. How far in advance can I book my honeymoon?

A. You can book your honeymoon approximately one year in advance. This limitation is primarily due to the airlines who typically do not have their schedules and prices more than one year in advance. In most instances though it is recommended that you start researching one year in advance and book your trip 6-9 months in advance.

Q. What should I plan on spending on my honeymoon and for how many days does the average person go away?

A. In 2000 the average honeymoon cost approximately $3,500.00 and the average length of stay was 7 nights. These numbers vary dependent upon your choice of resort and destination. Many people have gone to Las Vegas and reporting spending 4 nights and less then $1000 for four star resorts.

Q. We are both active and like to golf, play tennis, snorkel, go to the gym and want a beach. We are getting married in Atlanta and do not want to fly more than 3 hours. We also like good night life and are thinking about an "all inclusive" resort. One more thing, we don't want any kids at the resort, where would you suggest?

A. If your budget was approximately $3,500.00 then I would suggest looking at one of the Sandals Resorts or Grand Lido Resorts in Jamaica. These all-inclusive resorts will give you all you want plus more. For one price you will receive a package that includes your airfare, transportation to/from the hotel, meal, drinks and activities and they do not allow anyone under the age of 16 at either of these resorts.

Bizarre Questions and Beyond...

I am getting married soon and my father has had a sex change operation. I really want him/her to walk me down the aisle, but I don't know how to proceed. Help!

A. Please remember that the custom of walking the bride down the aisle and giving her away stems from ancient times when women were considered property. Nowadays it is not unusual for the bride to walk herself down the aisle. This option would cause the least amount of attention, since the focus should be on you and your groom and not on your biological father who has had a sex change.

Q. I am getting married this summer in a beautiful mountain meadow, with a gazebo. It will be very "natural" and casual. My fiancé wants to have his DOG as his best man! He says this dog IS his best friend. Since the ceremony is not in a house of worship, he feels it would be okay to have the dog in our wedding. What do you think?

A. Believe it or not, this is not the first time I've heard this! I have even heard of the dog "carrying" the rings in a pouch around its neck, wearing a bow-tie or a flower "tiara" depending on it's role as a groomsman/dog or bridesmaid/dog. You only go around once in this world, so dare to be different! Yours definitely will NOT be a traditional wedding, nor one to be easily forgotten! Just be sure the dog is well mannered...and trained! Good Luck!

Q. Our wedding reception is going to be in a very lovely VFW lodge. The problem is, the walls are covered in photos of dead veterans. I really don't want these old guys staring down at us during our reception. Any suggestions? The VFW lodge will not allow the photos to be removed.

A. I would suggest using tall trellises covered in ivy to place in front of the walls. If that doesn't work, perhaps there is a way you can drape gauzy material with ivy or flowers in front of the walls.

Q. My mother insists on wearing a white dress in my wedding. Not only is it white (like mine) but it is low-cut and has this weird stand-up collar at the back. She will look like Snow White and I will be mortified. What should I do?

A. I couldn't resist this…but I didn't use it in my answer (S.G.) *You could have your bridesmaids dress as the Seven Dwarfs.*

Your mother sounds like she has a dramatic flare! Is there someone of authority or someone your mother respects—clergy, sister, best friend, her mother—who could talk to her? If this isn't possible, I would suggest you write your mother a well-thought-out letter explaining your feelings…"Mom, you are so lovely and regal, you don't need such an over-done dramatic dress to make a statement. Besides, I don't really want to compete with you on my special day. Maybe you could choose another dress, with a more sophisticated, less dramatic, but becoming style."

Q. My fiancé wants to consummate our marriage on the limousine ride immediately after the ceremony. I'm not sure I want to do this. What do you think?

A. There's a good reason you are not sure you want to do this because a quickie in a limo is not the right time or place to consummate your marriage. Explain to your fiancé that this is not a woman's idea of a romantic rendezvous, nor does it show respect for your feelings as his future wife. Tell him you both will experience greater pleasure when you are completely alone and unhurried.

Q. I was wondering if I should be cool to the idea of having my fiancé's two ex-girlfriends stand up in our wedding. I feel a bit uncomfortable with the idea.

A. Of course you would! They need not stand up for your wedding, but as friends may be welcome guests.

Q. We are planning for the wedding party to ride from the church to the reception on motorcycles. What should we wear?

A. This all hinges on what you are planning to wear to the wedding and to the reception and if you want to take time to change your outfits. I would strongly suggest you NOT wear a wedding dress, even if you are a seasoned cycler and know how to ride side-saddle.

Q. Do you know or do you know anybody that could tell me the requirements for marriage to an inmate in Missouri?

A. I would check with the State Warden for accurate information.

Q. My fiancée's mother wants her lesbian companion to stand up with her at the wedding. My fiancée has difficulty in accepting the situation. My parents are very prim and proper. What should we do?

A. The brides' mother's companion in this case ought not to be considered her escort. She apparently does not have a long-standing relationship with your fiancée, nor does she have an official standing in the wedding party or the ceremony. She may be seated in the first row with the bride's mother. I suggest that you talk to your officiant before the wedding and let him/her explain.

Q. I was adopted as an infant and recently began corresponding with my birth mother, whom we haven't yet met, but who plans to attend my wedding. Where should she be seated and what about the dance?

A. I have discussed similar situations with others and the consensus is your biological mother ought to be introduced to the guests and treated as a "friend of the family". A close friend or relative ought to be assigned to her in order to make her feel welcome and comfortable. Your adoptive mother will be seated in the first row and your biological mother ought to be seated in the second row. The groom may ask her to dance sometime during the evening, after he has danced with the bride, the mother of the bride and his mother.

Q. We have recently received a wedding invitation and we have no idea who the people are that are getting married! We have asked all our relatives, friends and business associates and they can't help us. What should we do?

A. Try calling the hosts (parents of the bride) or one of the bridal couple's names on the invitation. Explain your mystery invitation and hopefully they will give you an answer. Perhaps your invitation was intended for someone else in the same city with the same name. Good luck!

Q. My father is going to give me away and perform the ceremony at my wedding (he is an ordained minister). The problem is this; we have never had a close physical relationship and he HATES to dance. I am finding that this is causing a huge deal of stress. We are both going to be very uncomfortable.

A. One way around the discomfort would be, rather than having all the 'specialty' dances done separately, have a wedding party dance. The DJ could announce you and your dad, and the groom and his mom to start the dance, after 1/2 minute or so ask the Best Man and Maid of Honor out to the floor, then the rest of the attendants. This way you'll never be in the spotlight which will help minimize the discomfort for both of you.

Q. Just wondering what seems to be the 'norm' at gay weddings or more precisely lesbian weddings— re: the dance choice.

A. At lesbian weddings for the slow dance music and songs many selections from any and all of the "crooner's," of the 50's and 60's remain popular. Some names? Sinatra, Sammy Davis, Dean Martin, Vic Damone, Tom Jones, Johnny Mathis, Tony Bennett, Elvis Presley, Engelbert

Humperdinck. Many lesbian women also love dancing to the Swing and Blues rhythms using the West Coast Swing as their dance favorite.

Q. We are having a medieval wedding and I am trying to find a way to learn a simple dance that is beautiful but not to complicated... any suggestions?

A. I have good news for you! The following link: http://www.pbm.com/ ~lindahl/del/ called *Del's Dance Book* will provide you with any and all information regarding medieval dancing. It shows the steps and then forms patterns. There is plenty of history and explanation.

Authors' Biographies

Sherri Goodall

Sherri Goodall knows from whence she speaks. She owned a party store for several years in Tulsa and was a sought after party planner. The ultimate test came when she planned her daughter's wedding in 1994. Utilizing her creativity to the maximum, she unearthed the most efficient and effective ideas and resources necessary to produce a wedding unique to the bridal couple...a wedding with panache, dazzle, sophistication and originality.

Goodall is the Editorial Advisor and a Contributing Editor for *Oklahoma Bride*, which debuted in January 1999.

In August of 1998, Goodall became a M.O.G. (mother of the Groom) and found that she could wear beige, but keeping her mouth shut was a stretch. (There is a well known maxim among wedding literati that mothers of the groom are expected to wear beige and keep their mouths shut.)

Goodall is a freelance writer, specializing in travel. Her articles have appeared in several publications including *Departures, Travel News,*

Tycoon, and *Aqua Magazines*.. She writes for *Tulsa People, Tulsa Kids, and Tulsa Woman*. An avid grandmother, Goodall has written several humorous essays on grandmotherhood, which have appeared in *50 Plus, Metrofamily, Nostalgia*, and *Senior Magazines*.

She has developed *M.O.B. Tools of the Trade* TM, workbook materials that she uses when she presents her her M.O.B. Workshops across the country. She can be queried about wedding planning questions on **www.weddingdetails.com**, or **www.bridesmom.com**.

"I have ridden elephants in Chiang Mai, tuk tuks in Bangkok, hot-air balloons over Kenya, camels in Eilat, rafts on the Colorado river, cabs in reverse in Mexico City (when the transmission ran in one direction only—reverse)," says Goodall, "but the most thrilling ride of all was the one in the elevator down to my daughter's wedding!"

She graduated with a Masters in fine arts and has had careers as a graphic artist, art therapist, art gallery owner, real estate agent, willing traveler, and participant in community activities. Sherri loves to explore new fields of endeavor and has recently taken tap dancing and boxing—neither of which threaten her "day job." She lives in Tulsa with her husband, two Westies, and a ceaseless imagination.

Edith Gilbert

Edith Gilbert has been called the "Amy Vanderbilt of the North" by Town and Country Magazine. As an arbiter of good taste and style, her entertaining is legendary.

She has answered over 12,000 tricky Wedding Etiquette Questions on www.weddingdetails.com. Many couples have replied with a sincere, "Thank you! Your answer was short, sweet and to the point!" and "You are wonderful to reply so quickly and so thoughtfully!!!"

She is the author of several books including, "The Complete Wedding Planner" which was first published in 1982, and has been revised and newly published in a third edition in 2001 as the "Official Know It All Wedding Planner". Mothers of the bride have called it their bible. The *Detroit Free Press* states, "It includes everything... savvy."

Edith, member of ABC (Association of Bridal Consultants" for 20 years, has been selective in acting as wedding consultant to a limited number of brides. Her feature articles have appeared in the *New York Times* and *Chicago Tribune* and have been nationally syndicated through the *United Featuers Syndicate*. She has been invited as a guest speaker to the annual conventions of the National Restaurant Association in Chicago, Ill., Special Events Magazine in Del Coronado, Ca., and to the Greenbrier in White Sulphur Springs, W. Va.

Her delightful new book, "Easy Entertaining", a part of the Official Know It All series published by Frederick Fell Publishers, Inc., will be available in spring of 2001. It covers the social scene for both casual entertaining at home to formal dining at gala events.

Edith's company, Jet'iquette, is a consultation service on dining and table setting for the hospitality trade. Her website is **www.charlevoix. org/edith.**

Lois Pearce Master Bridal Consultant

Lois developed her skill as a wedding consultant through the Association of Bridal Consultants, a trade organization for wedding professionals. After completing the levels of Professional Bridal Consultant and Accredited Bridal Consultant she attained the level of Master Bridal Consultant, one of 22 in the world. She serves as the Director of Ethnic Diversity and as the Connecticut State Coordinator of the Association of Bridal Consultants and is the Vice President - Membership of the New York Metro Chapter of the International Special Events Society

Her career began planning events for family and community organizations. Since starting Beautiful Occasions in 1986 she has assisted in weddings from Georgia to Massachusetts.

A recognized authority in the wedding industry, Lois has appeared on ABC, CBS, NBC and Public Television. She has been quoted in many of the major bridal publications, some of which include: *Brides and Your New Home, Modern Bride, Signature Bride* and *Bridal Guide.* Her assistance has been given to the *New York Daily News, Washington Post, Chicago Tribune* and other major newspapers. She is also quoted in "The Complete Idiot's Guide to Planning the Perfect Wedding" (Versions I & II), "The Portable Wedding Consultant", The Budget Wedding Sourcebook and "Going To the Chapel". Currently, *she serves on the* Editorial Advisory Board *of Signature* Bride *Magazine,* is an Instructor of "Really Getting Started", a bridal consultant training program and teaches courses in cultural diversity. Lois is the author of the "Ethnic and Specialty Wedding Guidebook" and is an Adjunct Professor of Gateway Community College.

Lois strives to make each occasion special down to the last details. Her goals are for each wedding to reflect the tastes of the client though the selections they are making for this very special day.

You can query Lois as to tradition and culture questions about wedding planning at www.weddingdetails.com.

"Ethnic and Specialty Wedding Guidebook" can be ordered direct from Beautiful Occasions, PO Box 185636, Hamden, CT., 06518.

Lois's website is **www.BeauOccsn@aol.com.**

Jeff Allen

Jeff Allen has been dancing since he was barely a teenager in the 1960's. He holds membership credentials with the North American Dance Teachers Association and the Pan-American Teachers Association. He also holds Associate credentials with the Imperial Society of Teacher of Dance.

Jeff turned professional in July 1984 after winning the Gold closed level at the North American Championships. He has won several Dance Championships including the New England Professional American Smooth Championship. He took a bold step in 1986 and added elements of the Argentine Tango style to his professional American Tango choreography. Today all top competitors in the American Smooth divisions use Argentine Tango to add drama to the American Style. Jeff's greatest pride is the more than 30 Top Teacher awards he has won in addition to keeping his position consistently in the list of the Top 75 teachers in North America.

In March 2000 Jeff Allen became a columnist for *Dancing USA Magazine*. Michael Fitzmaurice, Publisher/Editor of *Dancing USA Magazine* writes in the April/May 2000 issue:

"A new addition to the Dancing USA family is Jeff Allen, author of the hugely successful Quickstart to Dance series. Jeff possesses an encyclopedic mastery of dance technique, the ability to teach like your favorite professor and the skill to write like the best selling author he is…"

Mr. Allen is available on **www.weddingdetails**.com to answer your questions about dance. You can visit his website **www.quickstartbooks.com** for more information on his books, "Quickstart to Social Dancing", "Tango," "Swing," or his "Perfect Wedding Dance Instructional Video and Booklet," and "The Complete Guide to Slow Dancing."

Jeff is available for coaching, judging, and teaching. Toll free telephone 1-888-254-3162

Pat Taylor

Pat has been a professional photographer since 1969. He sold his very first photograph in that year to TWA while stationed at Pearl Harbor, Hawaii. After his tour with the U.S. Navy, Pat returned home to Cincinnati and opened Tru-Life Photography. At the peak of his wedding business, Pat and two part time photographers were covering over one hundred and fifty weddings a year. Since the very first wedding in 1972, Pat has photographed over one thousand weddings. Although his bridal couples are mainly from the southwestern Ohio area Pat travels all over the mid-west to provide creative wedding portraiture for his bride and grooms.

Pat lectures to many professional organizations and has been the invited guest speaker for Kodak at the Professional Marketing Associations annual international show in New Orleans and Las Vegas.

On the personal side, Pat has been married to Connie Judd Taylor for over twenty-three years and they have two children and two grandchildren. Pat is currently serving his first term on the Eaton City Council and was elected Mayor by his fellow council members.

Pat operates Pat Taylor Photography/Digital Imaging in Eaton, Ohio. He has a staff of four full time employees and has converted his studio operation to full digital capability as of March of 2000. The studio is opened six days a week and the mainstay of their business is high school senior portraits and related school photography.

Pat may be contacted at 937-456-5193 or faxed at 937-456-5068. His e-mail address is ptphoto@voyager.net and his web address is **www.pattaylorphoto.com**.

Jack Benoff

Jack Benoff has been involved in the travel industry for over 17 years. He founded a travel company that specialized in honeymoons. Jack has helped hundreds of couples choose the correct honeymoon location for their special journey. He has extensive knowledge of the Caribbean, cruises, and Hawaii.

Jack was president of a publishing company that specialized in consumer travel publications. He is presently a marketing consultant in the travel industry.

Notes

Notes

_____

_____

_____

_____

_____

_____

_____

_____

_____

_____

_____

_____

_____

_____

_____

_____

_____

Index

Order Form

WEDDINGDETAILS.COM FAQ's   Qty. _____ @ $8.95 $_____

NOTES FROM THE M.O.B.   Qty. _____ @ $12.95 $ _____

M.O.B., TOOLS OF THE TRADE   Qty. _____ @ $16.95 $ _____
(organizer and home file)   (no tax)

NOTES FROM THE M.O.B. and   Qty. _____ @ $26.00 $ _____
TOOLS OF THE TRADE... (SAVE 15%)

Shipping/handling: $ 3.50 1st item , $1.50 each addition item $ _____

Sales tax: (Oklahoma only) 7.917% (on books only) $ _____

TOTAL $ _____

Order online at Bridesmom.com, weddingdetails.com
Fill out order form and remit with:
❏ check ❏ money order, or charge by ❏ MasterCard or ❏ VISA

PENNYTHOUGHT PRESS
7512 So. Gary Place, Tulsa, OklA. 74136

Or order by telephone toll free 1 (877) 30 WORDS (309-6737), By fax (918) 491-2016

Name _____
Address _____
City_____State_____Zip_____

Card# _____ ❏ VISA ❏ MasterCard Exp. Date _____
Signature _____ Daytime phone (____) _____

Allow 2 -4 weeks for delivery. Prices subject to change without notice